AF421527

All rights reserved. No part of this book may be stored in a retrieval system, reproduced or transmitted in any form or by any other means without written perison from the publisher. Critics and reviewers may quote breif passages in connection with a review r critical article in any media.

aplombpub.co

isbn: 9789987057803
Written by: Daveen Eveline
Compiled by: Aplomb Publishing
Poetry art by: DarkBrushJars

Clock Words

TABLE OF CONTENTS

Shatter the image you have for love.
Instead ravage what you hide from yourself. Gather a
refection that can reveal your heart, Because only time will
tell such difference between love and its lustrous veil.

- Clock Words

As time has continued,
only now am I listening.
Her truth finally
louder than a whisper

Clock Words
ONLY TIME WILL TELL

KNIGHT

Blind is the effect of one's silence
And truth is the cause of opinion
But my true quiet question to you is
Why can't I let go easily
I can feel my fragile emotions fall
Slowly being built up at the same time
Can't you just close your eyes
With me
Hold me
See me
Understand me
Be only for me

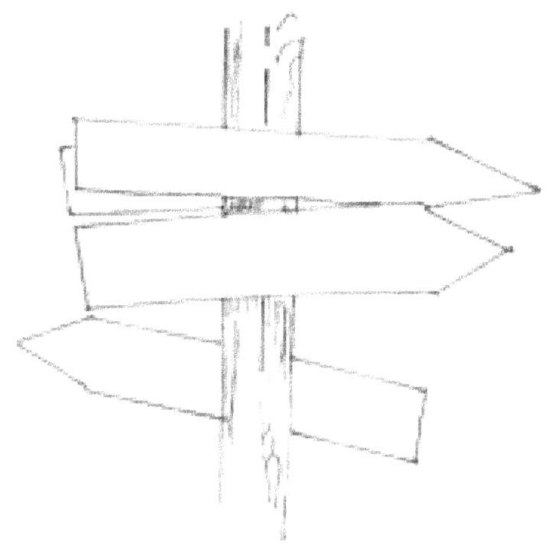

No?
It's not possible
Too many eyes from too many people
Opinions felt a mile away
My life becomes stay
I'm lost
Confused
And Loveless
Heatless
Even A bit clueless
But my life is much more sturdily built
It's built upon truth and desire
I am aware,
It's very fragile.

We have time for the Divine

And Spirit for the broken

We have divided the two

With words non·spoken

With breath both have

Yet one is stolen

With demand one needs

And demand one gets

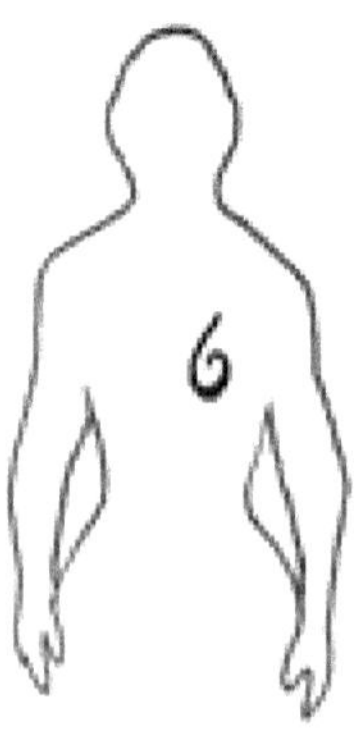

Only one is seen

And same is token

With love in my eyes

And hope in my heart

With faith in my hands

We shall not be torn apart

The sky is the limit they preach

Then why do we have stars

For this great divide

It's neither your burden nor ours

Written words
Mentally unwritten
Express verbs
Never became
Window scene
Heart pain
Disaster struck
A broken string
Only so many left
Before a blood stain
Love is powerful
But it's a strain
Who was meant to deal with trust
Love and lust
Loyalty and patience
It's too much

It's all too much
How can one be loved
Flaws shown and discussed
Expressed and written
She's a feline
A Queen
No!
A kitten?
Can you please revealed to me this art
I've never painted something so dark
I can't see this canvas
Rivers block my view
It's hard to understand
I know
But all I want
Is to be loved by you

You always ask me why.
I always say I don't know.
But if I have to pick any reason,
It would be because...
I love you and here's why.
Even after my cowardly break up,
Years flew by and I still knew your name.
Time has passed and I still feel that pain.
Days continue to fast forward
Still there's thoughts of you in my brain...

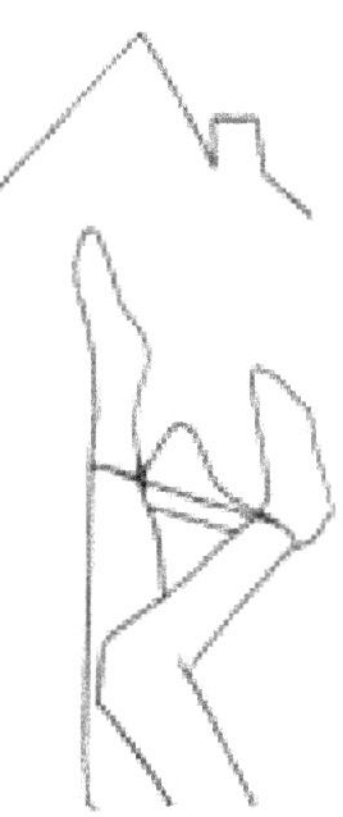

From height to humor.
From smiles to smirks
From love to leaving .
From house to hoes.
Even from Bride to Bros.
You're still there in my thoughts.
And I lied before,
I know why we were no more.
My friends helped me escape.
A prison idea that they had made.
I followed their path.
Their reasons and beliefs.
But if it wasn't for me,
Listening to the heart that wasn't mine.
You and I would still certainly be a we.

Popularity
Isn't it funny... she says she likes me.

unknowingly i couldn't have guessed
you were such a masterpiece
letting myself think you wouldn't look my direction
it's just that one smile that made my week
all i could remember
was my red sweatshirt
and now every time i see it i smile all over again
when i think of you
i see such a wonderfully amazing smile
i dream of the nights when i'm going to be in your arms
i see a future with you Mr.C
only if i could have such a remarkable chance
to get to know you
rather than to keep dreaming off of looks and possibility
you should be aware of my difference
between love and lust
for you my darling
i lust for you

why must one acquire pride receiving a confession
what be the reason they perform less affection
ignoring the face of their potential one
damn you, conversing about my unrequited love
but in silence hiding the mutuality
we are all human, true
but we are not all a being
one with love, control, and self-esteem
if you love her, then tell her
if you don't
never forget
pain of the heart is real
just as the pain you will soon feel
because your words mean something to her
sadly, meaningless to karma
but in other words
speak as you do but make it the truth
because your words can have honor
till they don't
think about it
what is a heart that is blue
a soul that is glued
and a man without his word
it's a bumpkin, that is you
without a clue, remaining to one side

now you are viewed with expensive dishonor
Ha, what a laughable phrase

have you ever gained interest and lost it
question people about it
have you ever ate something and loved it
and tried it again and be disgusted
have you ever looked at someone and thought
you are the most beautiful creature i have ever laid eyes on
but when you're not by them their just some person
or even be thinking about someone
then start to question why
hmmmmmm, can you please just get out of my head
these are the words yelled to yourself, correct?
i think i wink i blink i cross
over the thought of even questioning you
if i ask you a question in real life instead of in my head
can i think or fathom if you would rather be dead instead
answer this question of mine

yes, you, Mr. over there i've ignored for the last time
check your watch check your clock check your phone tic-toc
my questions are real very sustained
my questions are truly legit
Held together with curiosity and riddles, every bit...
riddle me this
 you have something that all obtain
except different in multiple ways
it grows and grows every day
but to me, a stranger, it is a mystery
i question and question with my own in place
this thing we all have but different in our human race
still to ourselves it is a questioned masterpiece
with these clues in mind think of what all humans have
it's grow, that friends know, and strangers wait to discover
ha, as ourselves we are waiting with them
so what makes you a stranger to yourself ?
perhaps one's own personality.

17

One Hitters

This goes out to the guy
That I will never know why
When I had no sight
Fell for his voice
It was my first day at a new school
I was alone and he was so cool
When I came into this class
Questions, and people asking them bypassed
But all I remember hearing
Is something about a slushie and a 7/11
Now this was a time I had pain
I was truly broken and couldn't relate
But when I left that day
I stumbled into him and saw his eyes
I was still glassesless and blind
But I was so close I saw them shine
The color so bright
And that encounter made my day and my night
Not because he was cute
But because I just knew
One day we might be friends
But now those days are near
And I must realize I shouldn't steer
Because knowing me
We're gonna crash
Because I can't think at the sight
Because I am a true believer
If I want something I drive straight for it
And i've heard you don't like chocolate...ice cream?
So why waste my time to fill up the tank
Just to run out of gas at an intersection
Oh, and you and your girl, yall cute
Adorable even

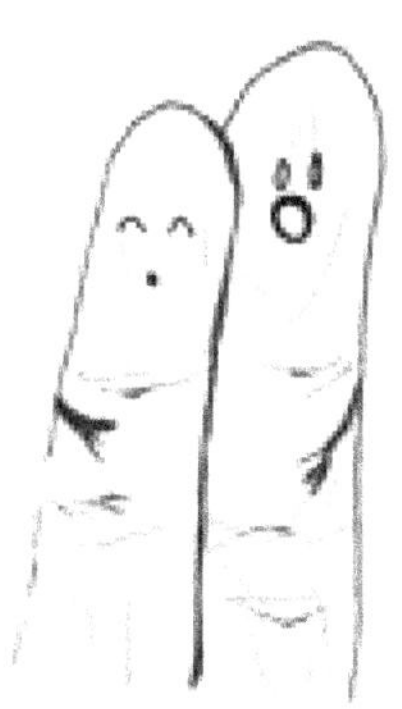

When I looked into your eyes
Which I do every chance I get
I see a friend
And a guy, that's just super cute
Adorable
Handsome
And a gentlemen
I see someone that would go to 7/11 and buy a slushie
I see you
Someone with nothing but good vibes
Someone kind hearted and trustworthy
But I must confess, when I graduate
You're the one I wish i had a chance
And indeed to apologize as well
For all who may know whom I'm referring
If you yourself have figured it out
It's not that hard actually
I think you're cute and kind
I seriously doubt that you would mind
Oh and you should be aware
Every chance I get I let people know
I tell them that you are eyecandy
You have such beautiful curly hair
And a beautiful singing voice too
I just thought you should know

you love me then you don't
you held me now you won't
you looked at me then away
what's wrong i wonder
is it me
is it you
or is it the fact of us
i can't believe this
once again i don't know what i missed
i knew what you were thinking
for now i guess,
it's just a ship sinking

Hold me I ask
Kiss me I ask
But it's too much for me and you
I love you stupid thru it's grains
Love is difficult to the fullest
Love is selfish and hard to destroy
Love is what love is

It's the parasite in my mind
It grows and grows
Once it's there I'm it's slave
The only thing love can never control
Is the person,
In which its person Is in love with

Love enemy is hatred and hatred is easy to rid of
The only problem hatred works faster than love
Love is harder to dismiss than hatred
I hate that I love you, too bad I don't know what I mean

I refuse to give you a part of me
Because in the end it's a waste of my beauty
If I welcomed you in
With all of your mystery
I'm creating a path
For you to leave history
I love you not
And wish to never will
Your handsome side
Has yet been truly revealed
But your beastly frenz
I know too well
Due to your nice vocals and words
I've welcomed a kiss
From a man that'll never be mine
Yet he still bother's hers
This pains me, even the slightest thought
Because your beauty and words marked me so
Im too far in to push you away
And to be honest I don't even think I want to
Because you're invading me
So, how about you just leave

Mister Mister you are fine
Probably taste like a glass of wine
Your aspirations difficult to discover
But your tendency all the covered
Your eyes may show passion
But our relationship showed vexation
Still you are handsome
And the thought of your body, my distraction
Mister Mister you are fine
But blind in the face of life
You are lost in time not required
I think your mind has lost its desire
Still, I will always see you as Mister Mister
The boy who didn't quite understand himself
Yet, his eyes showed how he felt
His smile would make any girl melt
Even though I did not actually know YOU
Dreams, Nightmares, and Wishes
My words still sound, at ease, and tranquil
Because Mr. Mr. you could've been mine
If you were honest before we lost our time.

BITTERSWEET

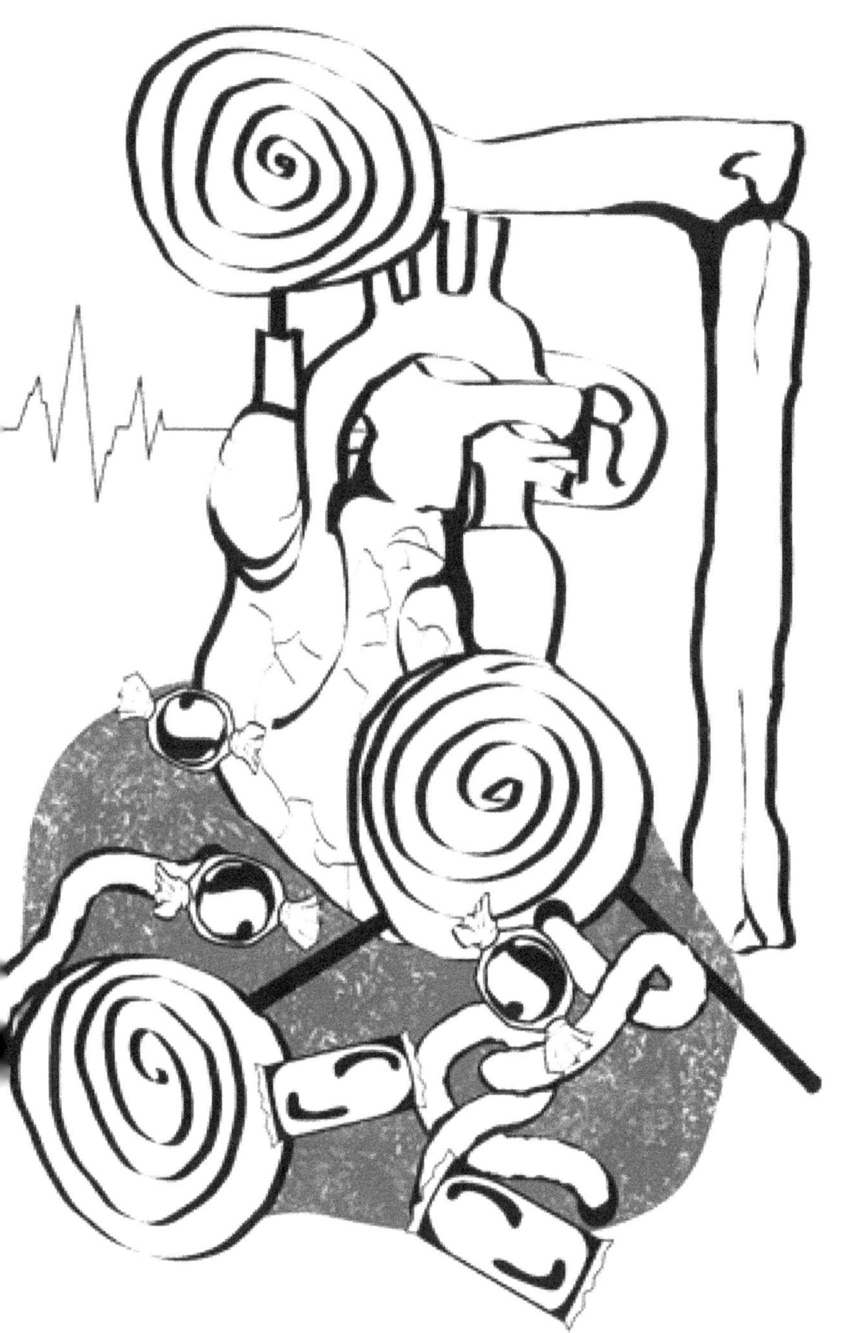

I was so overwhelmed by your appearance
I began to change myself to fit into your crazy world
It seemed as though you accept my intention
Believe me it's not misguided
Perhaps an alternate perception
But your silence is making my mind implode
I have no idea why you intrigue me
The fact that I'm interested whispers daydreams
Although I do fear this
One day our friendship will be a myth
And our ship sinks
Conversations will cease
And we will no longer be friends
We will become strangers

Watching the same tides
From different sides
Dreaming on the same island
Thinking with our discombobulated minds
And never seeing one another again in time
There is no fault
When I don't know
I tend to drift away
Only because I feel I will be safe
And as I sink I change
And restore to the girl you met first before
Waking up on a new island
Hoping that this time
My mind will lay rest
My soul less depressed
My heart more affectionate
And my memories less apparent
Also, my thoughts of you ...
I would have to hope become less vivid

You're not mine
You're not bae
The more and more we talk
The less I can say
Your fun is fun
I feel for you and of you

But of course my silence never loudens
I could speak of a relationship
But what would be the point
To talk as we do now
Another story shall be written
One with a happy ending

If I could tell you in person
   I love you
        Because I do, I would
             Still your silence isn't very welcome
                  I need you to speak and display

Show me I have the potiental to be the one
     Good night, Sweet dreams and How was your days
        It's not enough

But my silence still remains
Only because your sight is stained
So I choose to paint
Write, Read, expressed in a form of Art
Your silence lives for days

Mine shall be portrayed
So goodnight, sweet dreams
I refuse to stay
This is the end of our days
Me and you will go separate ways

when you stated the idea of making love
i knew your truth
but accepted your lie anyway
my blind affection for you saw no wrong
i just want to know the feeling
what's it like

i've never felt that feeling
the feeling i reach for with plight
inside me it's supposed to be great
hormones will riot and passion will stay
moans and screams i preform
but not from memory

your eyes on my bodest
fabrics on the floor
the way i hope youll look at me with all my nudity
my presumptuous chest and belly with skin so soft
my long braids restraint less and free

my body's reveal and my shyness mistaken
my emotions on the run, frightened and misplaced
my desire for this action far too dreamt
i hope your body is as my mind assumes
i hope your eyes see my body
then your lips smile

38

i really wish that your hands,
touch my body completely
without personal restraint or retreat
i hope the insecurity i see and feel, you never notice

i hope my aura darkness doesn't disturb us
i hope my emotional walls won't tumble
because what i desire could cause a rumble
the hormones aren't the only on the rise
my emotions would be too i might cry

i truly feel this action be my undoing
not because i want it
but because i want you

God I beg
Bring me somebody that desires my time
Intrigue about my grind
Holds me tight, someone who's all mine

God just bring me him
The one that rolls up just to say hi
The one that picks me up just to ride
The one that kisses me without goodbye

God bring me truth
My one burning desire
The man that'll bring me higher
Someone to hold me with my weights

The one that'll never leave
Never hate
The one that I'll give my love too

My actual heart
My actual full attention
Without pain
Without suffering

Without walking backwards
Without running
Without staying still
Without worry

Without the thought
That I'm wasting my time
Trying to figure him out

you
always
ask
me
why
And I never have a good answer
I joke I joke I play and I pry
iIn't it good enough that you're just a good guy
I call I text I think about my ex
I ponder I worry I question your mind
I feel I hurt I gather confidence and became an extrovert
I can't I can I would I won't
Call you and tell you I love you, but you don't
I can't but I do feel your pain to you

I want to but I can't understand what you've been through
                    You love, You brush, You move forward
                    But still look back at us
Our past, the plane of just us
                              Ha, you think you can't relate?
                                    My love no my lust
                    Your eyes no your last
Your crush yes your past
                         the we
                         the us
                         the become
                         the one

He held onto me so tight
It was like he loved me.

He had only met me once or twice
Knowing that our lives are minced
Not nice
We knew of one another's heart not at all.

Yet could understand one another's pain all the same
Seemed to leave all the pressure, that's built up, behind
When it rains and your already blind.

As we race to a place with no one else
The heavens filled our sight
Mine with love
And his with the pain of his plight.

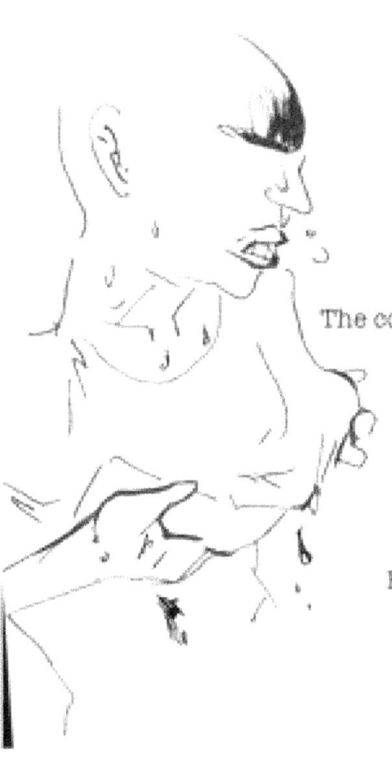

The cold drops of rain filled our clothes
The weight unnoticed.

Talking him up
He holds me close.

But soon as I squeeze a bit tighter
I feel his grip get lighter.

I hear his last sob
And his eyes I couldn't find.

My presence felt unwanted
But by the time I noticed he had already let go.

I just
I just don't understand
You are so handsome
But yet you say different
You tell me these truths
And I don't dismiss you because of them
I accept you
I wish for no change
None whatsoever
Because
I love your hair
And the sound of your voice
The way you walk
And how you interact with others
But now

Now I'm beginning to dislike you
I'm starting to think I mattered never
Because you are too typical
Such same
I'm very disappointed
Not because you don't like me
But because you pretended that you did
We were never friends
I was a simple target
Now that I've removed it from my ladybit's
You act as though you see me not
Ok.
I'm blind of your beautiful sight as well
It'll be mutual

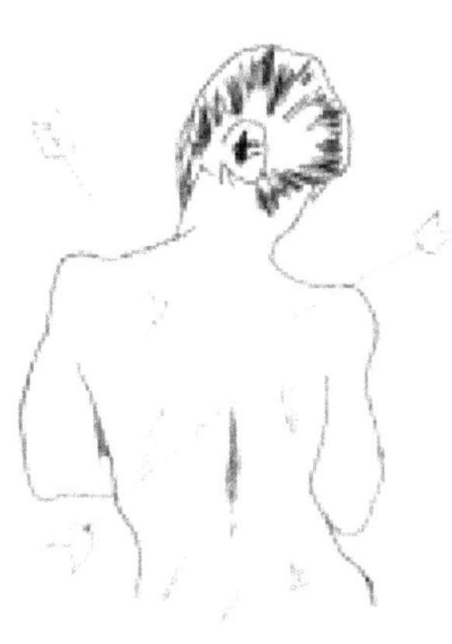

I just
I just don't understand
You are so handsome
But yet you say different
You tell me these truths
And I don't dismiss you because of them
I accept you
I wish for no change
None whatsoever
Because
I love your hair
And the sound of your voice
The way you walk
And how you interact with others
But now

Now I'm beginning to dislike you
I'm starting to think I mattered never
Because you are too typical
Such same
I'm very disappointed
Not because you don't like me
But because you pretended that you did
We were never friends
I was a simple target
Now that I've removed it from my ladybit's
You act as though you see me not
Ok.
I'm blind of your beautiful sight as well
It'll be mutual

I accidentally tripped
And you fell into my heart
I gripped it tight
Scared it might fall apart
I looked within
Only took a peek

The rush flooded
The thought of you and me
I tend to do this
This wild thing
Fall in love
Without first expressing

But still this I
The one I'm becoming
Wanted to reveal the treasure
But when I reached for your hand
I realized
You never let go of the other

I felt unworthy
Uncomfortable
I can't explain this weakness
You'd just gently hold my feelings
I can't love like everyone
So I distance from my sharp parts

Quietly I've just added this torment
Added to my shattered heart
I created a secret within
Stupidly,this lost, a feeling uneven
And precise distance
I pushed
I desire your mind body and soul

To grasp your ideals and make them real
I wish to finally be the woman for someone
And not just myself anymore
However
I've got to accept
You've already found somebody
Somebody now to do that with

Things I think
But I don't say
I love your touches
I wish I felt them in more places
I love your smile
I wish I could make you mine
I love your humor
It intrigues me immensely
I lust for your embrace
Wish for your lips to taste

Forever
Eternity
Vast
Abyss
The empty
I'm ok with filling it with you

My fears
Frights
Plights
Problems
And insecurities
I hope they subside

I can decide
I've decided
I'm ok with falling in love with you
All I ask
Please be greater than the idea you have presented

I can love you
I feel it within
I'll push aside my worries
Just for you to be mine
I fear nothing
I love all
And you my dear
Please catch me when I fall

Why do I feel scum
For wanting your body in mine

Where's the decision
Her love or mine

Why when I decide to ignore her presence
I feel selfish and undeserving

How come I decided to love you
And every second you don't tell me that you want me too, I hurt

Why don't you want me
Is it my body you've decided upon

That's so purposeless

If I was blind I'd love your soul through touch
If I was deaf I'd love your soul with every waking moment
If I was mute our love language world speak for centuries

I'm so uncertain
I'm so undecided
I've become concerned
About my selfish intent

I could say I love you because of this feeling
Yet that's most of nothing compared to how I feel

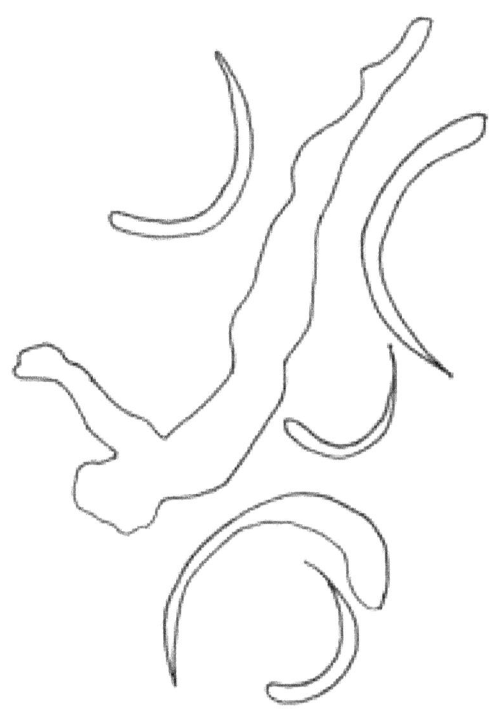

Just let go of your safety net dear

I swear I'll catch you, I'm right here

You are so you
I am so me
We aren't a we
The realization is so heavy

This weight that I've agreed
Is beginning to drown me in the deep sea
The water of our future
The one apparently only created by me

The ship I built
Yet you never found
Instead you took another cruise
While I just waited around
I cry from my hearts ded
this sting from my heart strings

Anyway, this process I know repeat
I can lock my emotions
Caged
This numb I've now created
No pain
I'm ready to sail away
But
I'm dedicated to not leave you, okay
Wiping away my pain
I grab my weighted love, overboard I go
I'll float back to the top
If my love for you ever erodes

Look from my heart
With crystal eyes
Strummed love strings
Beats skipped
Words delivered
Touch accepted
Time desired
Company appreciated
Still
I feel not quite loved
Not quite lust
Limbo I rock within
Uncertain
Strange love for you
Yet attempt to maintain distance
Close is a dream
Cosmos diverge
I'm worth more than this feeling
Yet
I sin for you
I slowly die with every realization
I am not yours
And you belong to someone else
I desire our growth
But I dig the roots back up every time I set them
I cannot become grounded by you

Yet I replant myself when I think of you
Yanking the roots when I think of her
This process is hurtful
Yet
I sin for you
My eyes on your body
Hands on your parts
Lips on your lips
And mind in our future
We to be we yet our our is dim
This light you shine for us is bright
It feeds
I grow
Then I am rooted not
Desiring more
Accepting this crumb role
It's below me
My royal status laughed among
My lady revoked
2nd branded
And it hurts
Because
I accepted it

Does he love me
Or love me not
Petal
Petal
Petal
Eyes open I see you
Your smile
Hear your laugh
Funny you be
Handsome you are
Happy you have
This I strive
Touch I desire
Love I live to find
Within your grasp
Our time stands still
Infinite kisses you give, I take
Eternity I burn for you, yearn for you
Like none other
I want to hold your hand
Kiss your lips
Allow you to be mine
Tell me
Petal
Petal
Petal
Love me
Or love me not
Am I enough for you
You certainly are for me
In every way

After time spent
Well aquatinted

        Friendship grew
       Could never sank it

              Sailed the blue
             Sky turned dark

       Secrets filled the ship
      Laughter and laughter

We are royalty
Lust too pure

       Given a high dosage
     YOU od'ed and thought frantic

       I whispered my strength into your eyes
           You saw more of me

     Then dropped your disguise
    Leaping overboard you never asked

But Yes you
I am the doctor and I prescribed you right

    All alone the ship sank without the flames
Our heat, the ships coals is nothing more than decoration

         As I drown lost in blind sight
          My crown is still mine

     And I'll forever hold it tight
     Farewell King

For I am still royalty
My apologies to you

      For ANY discrepancies

I created this picture
Framed with you
Captured by life
Shot by view
Shown to all
Except who knew
You loved me not
Damn boo hoo
Wait don't pause
Keep ahead to the applause
I thank you
For showing me the truth
Friendship is more than time spent
It's is made up of more than me and you
It's sad to say right now
But when I looked back at this canoe
You stopped paddling and faded in view
Farewell into the mist
Because I thought I knew
Now that I know you
I know you saw the same too

Situation presented
Direction ignored
Distracted by lust
Decisions were made
Love burst in my heart
Attacked by a man
His eyes filled with temptation
I was nothing more than a moment

Used for the time
Yet he committed no crime
Tears bleed from my eyes
Still friendship prevailed
Because love is stronger in my mind
I asked for you never to leave me
Still you drifted away
Stuck with me through thick and thin
But the ache you caused

How do I love this man
I decided to love you
This answer you demanded
Admiring you much so
My body was granted
My words pierced through my heart
But to you they were nothing more than standard
I wanted to love you forever
Once I asked for your love
Your decision I demand

Yet I never spoke this question
Instead I gave you an option
Silly me I said such
Words I meant none
I deserve you and your body to be mine
Yet I say, "if you want to love another, that's ok."
I scream inside saying theses words
That's why I shake
My nerves uneasy
Because I knew you'd never choose me
A side chick in truth
Yet blindly believing in you

Poems

yes, you, Mr. over there i've ignored for the last time
check your watch check your clock check your phone tic-toc
my questions are real very sustained
my questions are truly legit
Held together with curiosity and riddles, every bit...
riddle me this
 you have something that all obtain
except different in multiple ways
it grows and grows every day
but to me, a stranger, it is a mystery
i question and question with my own in place
this thing we all have but different in our human race
still to ourselves it is a questioned masterpiece
with these clues in mind think of what all humans have
it's grow, that friends know, and strangers wait to discover
ha, as ourselves we are waiting with them
so what makes you a stranger to yourself ?
perhaps one's own personality.

A Kings Patience
She wasn't ready to be loved
But of your king mentality
All you saw was her greatness and beauty
Her pain wasn't in your sight
So you loved, you wished she'd seen
Only if he knew
She was aware they were both royalty
Yet and still her crown slipped
And she refused his help to straiten it
Because she knew deep inside
The only one to fix herself
Is herself
And only then will she began to feel worthy
Only then could she accept her flaws and be loved by another
Not only because she felt her walls building too high
But because she fixed them
By taking them down
And all whom crowded her during her flood
She seeks forgiveness
For she not only was sorry but never loved them
Her pain was someone's lesson
Her decision to reign was her blessing

I'm sorry for my nature
My nurture never gifted
My love never had
My worth never received
So my burden be me
Because that's how I see
I'm currently removing these lenses
I'm attempting to be released
But to give surgery upon oneself is morally wrong
Still, last time someone had the scalpel
It was without anesthesia
Cutting deep
Scaring my stringed heart
It became so fragile
Now, I overthink
I'm aware of myself though
I forgive this unlicensed doctor
And your patience, admirable
So .... anyway·

I don't know how to rid myself of this pain
No line of words can describe
No amount of oxygen can support my lungs
This suffocation is deep
This wall is tall
This field is vast with no end
This empty is full
This negative is positive
The strength is broken with no means of a fix
This is more than depression
This is the worst
This is the pain
This is the stain
This is such hurt
This is and had no real words
You will not feel what I feel right now in this very moment
My pain can never become yours
Just as yours can never become mine
This pain is a passionate one
And there is no getting rid of passion even if it hurts
Music brings it out at a steady pace
So that I can return it to it's locked away place

When my pain leaks my capability does too
Ease my pain some ask
All I want is someone to bring me more happiness then I have gathered in pain.
That's all.
Somebody love me more than I hate myself
Somebody love me more than my hate for this pathetic life
Somebody please just love me more than my mother ever did
Somebody love me more than my father
More than my siblings
More than my grandma
Just love me more than my pain.
Just love my pain away.
Please somebody.

What's a promise ?
                    A word
What does it do?
                Give assurance
For what?
            Any and everything
Who needs that?
                    People
What kind of people?
            The kind that only had
                broken promises
How do you break a promise?
                    You lie
Why would someone wanna lie to the person
they're trying to give assurance to?

                I don't know

shoutout to all ex's who were never actually ex's

www.ingramcontent.com/pod-product-compliance
Lightning Source LLC
Chambersburg PA
CBHW041210150726
48006CB00016B/2196